KOBE BRYANT
MENTALITY

BECOME AS RELENTLESS AS A BLACK MAMBA
BY DECODING THE PSYCHOLOGY OF A

LEGENDARY LAKER:
KOBE BRYANT

-

CREATED BY
ETERNIA PUBLISHING

Kobe Bryant Mentality: Become As Relentless As A Black Mamba By Decoding The Psychology Of A Legendary Laker: Kobe Bryant
by ETERNIA PUBLISHING

Author: ETERNIA PUBLISHING
Contact: (contact@eterniapublishing.com)

If you liked the book, recommend your friends to download their own copy, thank you very much for respecting the author's work!

CONTENT

MENTAL TOUGHNESS FOR OVERCOMING STRUGGLE

How To Use Your Struggles To Shape Your Goals?
How To Use Your Suffering To Create Your Killer Instinct?
How To Have Your Head In The Game?
How To Keep Going?
Can Loneliness Be A Good Thing?
How To Change Your Perspective When You Suffer Because Things Don't Go Your Way?

MENTAL TOUGHNESS FOR LEADERSHIP

How Can A Basketball Team Be Good?
How To Handle A Team's Stubbornness?
Why Let Others Use Their Strengths Even When You're Good Enough?
Why Must A Leader Be Compassionate And Empathetic?
How Can A Team Be Good Year After Year?
Why Must You Be Honest With People?
How Must A Leader Train Their Team?

CONSISTENCY

How To Gain Real Consistency?
Why Rest At The End?
What Is Commitment?
Do You Need Constant Mentorship To Be Successful?

FAILURE

What Is Failure?
How To Recover From Failure?

PASSION

Why Must You Do What You Love To Do?
What To Do When You Retire?
How To Make Your Dreams Come True?
How To Stick To Your Dreams?
How To Choose Your Future Wisely Based On Your Passion?

ABOUT KOBE BRYANT

Kobe Bean Bryant was an American basketball player who played the shooting guard position. He was born on August 23, 1978, in Philadelphia, Pennsylvania, and passed away on January 26, 2020, in Calabasas, California. He participated in 20 NBA seasons, all of which he spent playing for the Los Angeles Lakers.

He is regarded as one of the greatest basketball players of all time and is the son of former basketball star Joe Bryant. He was an eighteen-time All-Star, fifteen-time All-NBA selection (eleven of them in the first five), twelve-time member of the best defensive quintets, MVP of the season in 2008, MVP of the Finals in 2009 and 2010, and the league's leading scorer in 2006 and 2007. He also won two Olympic gold medals with the United States national team. He also won five NBA championships with the Lakers and two with the national team. He received a posthumous induction into the Basketball Hall of Fame in the year 2020.

Bryant entered the NBA directly out of Lower Merion High School in Philadelphia in 1996, the year he was chosen by the Charlotte Hornets in the Draft but was later transferred to the Los Angeles Lakers. Between 2000 and 2002, he and Shaquille O'Neal led his squad to three straight NBA championships. Bryant took over as the Los Angeles team's lone star after O'Neal left in 2004, and between 2005 and 2007 he broke numerous scoring records. He guided the Lakers to back-to-back championships in 2009 and 2010 after they lost the Finals in 2008. His career was plagued by injuries in the last few years, and he decided to retire at the conclusion of the 2015–16 campaign.

The 81 points Bryant scored against the Toronto Raptors in January 2006 are the second-highest scoring output in NBA history, trailing only Wilt Chamberlain's 100 points in 1962. Bryant is currently ranked fourth on the list of all-time leading scorers in the NBA, both during the regular season and playoffs.

The Lakers retired his number 8 and number 24 jerseys on December 18, 2017, marking the first time in NBA history that a team did so for a single player. On the same day, Glen Keane's short video "Dear Basketball," in which he visually narrated the letter he published in The Players' Tribune to announce his retirement, was shown. The best animated short film category at the Oscars went to this movie.

In a helicopter crash in Calabasas, California, on January 26, 2020, he and eight other people (including the pilot) perished, including his 13-year-old daughter Gianna Maria. He was 41 years old.

EARLY LIFE

The only son of Pamela Cox Bryant and former NBA player Joe Bryant, Bryant was born in Philadelphia as the youngest of Pamela Cox Bryant's three children. Additionally, he was John "Chubby" Cox, an NBA playermaternal ,'s nephew. His parents gave him the name "Kobe beef" because they had seen it on a menu at a restaurant. His father's nickname "Jellybean" inspired the creation of his middle name, Bean. Bryant was raised a practicing Catholic since his family was.

When Bryant was a little child, he began playing basketball, and the Lakers were his favorite team. When Bryant was six years old, his father left the NBA and relocated his family to Rieti, Italy, where he now plays basketball professionally. After two years, they relocated to Pistoia, Reggio Emilia, and eventually Reggio Calabria. Kobe adapted to his new way of life and developed his fluency in Italian. His favorite childhood memories were created at Reggio Emilia, which he believed to be a lovely location. When Bryant was a resident in Reggio Emilia, he started taking basketball seriously. Bryant's grandpa would send him NBA game tapes so he could watch them and learn. He gained further basketball knowledge through animated sports movies from Europe, which served as another source of inspiration. His father competed for Olimpia Basket Pistoia from 1987 to 1989, teaming up with former Detroit Pistons Leon Douglas. Douglas said that Kobe worked as a ball boy and mop boy at the games and practiced shooting at intermission "Halftime at each of our games included the Kobe show. He would go outside and line up his shot. At halftime, we would have to eject him from the floor after coming out of the locker room ".

Bryant picked up the game of soccer and had AC Milan as his favorite team. Bryant would return to the country in the summer to participate in a basketball summer league. When Bryant was 13 years old, his family returned to Philadelphia, and he enrolled in Bala Cynwyd Middle School for eighth grade.

HIGH SCHOOL (1992–1996)

While attending Lower Merion High School in Ardmore, a Philadelphia suburb, Bryant had an outstanding high school career that brought him national acclaim. As a freshman, he participated in basketball on the varsity squad. Bryant started for Lower Merion's varsity squad for the first time in many years, although the group concluded with a 4-20 record. Bryant played all five positions for the Aces over the team's 77-13 record over the next three years. He received attention from college recruiters during his junior year when he averaged 31.1 points, 10.4 rebounds, 5.2 assists, 3.8 blocks, and 2.3 steals. He was voted Pennsylvania Player of the Year and was nominated for the fourth team of the Parade All-Americans. His top choices were Duke, Michigan, North Carolina, and Villanova. Bryant started to consider turning pro right after high schooler Kevin Garnett was selected in the first round of the 1995 NBA draft.

Bryant won the 1995 senior MVP honor at the Adidas ABCD Camp while competing with future NBA teammate Lamar Odom. Bryant played one-on-one with Jerry Stackhouse as a high school player in a scrimmage organized by the 76ers' then-coach John Lucas. Bryant led the Aces to their first state title in 53 years during his final year of high school. He led the Aces to a 31-3 record over the stretch, averaging 30.8 points, 12 rebounds, 6.5 assists, 4 steals, and 3.8 blocked shots. With 2,883 points at the conclusion of his high school career, Bryant surpassed Wilt Chamberlain and Lionel Simmons to hold the record for the most points scored in Southeastern Pennsylvania.

For his exceptional work during his final year at Lower Merion, Bryant won a number of accolades. These includes being recognized as the Gatorade Men's National Basketball Player of the Year, the Naismith High School Player of the Year, a McDonald's All-American, a first-team Parade All-American, and a member of the USA Today All-USA First Team. Greg Downer, Bryant's varsity coach, called him "a complete player who dominates" and lauded his work ethic despite being the team's star performer. Bryant invited R&B artist Brandy to his senior prom in 1996. Bryant, at 17, ultimately decided to enter the NBA right away, making him just the sixth player in NBA history to do so.

When Bryant's announcement first broke, there weren't many prep-to-pro NBA players, so it received a lot of attention (Garnett being the only exception in 20 years). He would have been admitted to any institution of his choice because to his basketball prowess and 1080 SAT score, but he never made an official school tour. Bryant was recognized as one of the 35 Greatest McDonald's All-Americans in 2012 for both his high school play and subsequent successes.

PROFESSIONAL CAREER

1996 NBA DRAFT

Bryant worked out in Los Angeles before to the 1996 NBA Draft, sparring with ex-Lakers Larry Drew and Michael Cooper. Then-Laker general manager Jerry West said that Bryant "marched over these individuals."

To open up salary cap room so they could make an offer to free-agent center Shaquille O'Neal, the Lakers were seeking to sell their starting center Vlade Divac in exchange for a player's draft rights. The day before the draft, according to Bill Branch, then-head scout for the Charlotte Hornets, the Hornets and Lakers agreed to trade the No. 13 choice. The Hornets had never thought about picking Bryant before the trade deal. Minutes before the decision was made at the draft, the Lakers gave the Hornets advice on who to choose. The first guard selected right out of high school was Bryant. When Divac vowed to retire rather than be dealt from Los Angeles after the draft, the transaction was placed in risk. However, Divac backed down from his ultimatum on June 30, and the deal became official on July 9, 1996, when the league's off-season ban came to an end. Bryant's parents had to cosign his contract with the Lakers since he was just 17 at the time; he wasn't old enough to sign it on his own until he turned 18 just before the start of the season. Bryant agreed to a $3.5 million, three-year rookie deal.

NATIONAL TEAM CAREER

Due to his impending marriage during the off-season, Bryant refused to participate in the 2000 Olympics. Additionally, he made the decision to skip the 2002 FIBA World Championship. After having arthroscopic operations on his shoulder and knee, Bryant withdrew from the 2003 FIBA Americas Championship. Due to his sexual assault conviction, he was forced to leave the Olympic squad the following summer. He was one of the first two players, along with LeBron James, publicly selected to the preliminary U.S. roster for the 2006–2008 season by Jerry Colangelo in 2006. But after knee surgery, he was sidelined once again and missed the 2006 FIBA World Championship.

Bryant's tenure with the American national team formally started in 2007. He competed for the 2007 USA Men's Senior National Team, which went 10-0, won gold, and qualified the American men for the 2008 Olympics. He also played for the USA FIBA Americas Championship Team. All 10 of the USA's FIBA Americas Championship games saw him start. In the competition, Bryant averaged 15.3 points, 2.9 assists, 2.0 rebounds, and 1.6 steals per game.

He was chosen to the 2008 Summer Olympics' USA Men's Senior National Team on June 23, 2008. He had never attended the Olympics before. Bryant scored 20 points, including 13 in the fourth quarter, along with six assists, as Team USA beat Spain 118–107 in the gold medal game on August 24, 2008, earning its first gold medal in a global tournament since the 2000 Olympics. While shooting, he had an average of 15.0 points, 2.8 rebounds, and 2.1 assists. 8 Olympic competitions saw 462 field goals made.

For the 2012 Summer Olympics, Bryant re-joined the national squad. Bryant made the decision to leave the squad after capturing another gold medal. He concluded his term with the national team with a 26-0 record across three competitions, taking home a gold medal each time.

PLAYER PROFILE

Bryant was a shooting guard who predominantly played. He was described as being 212 pounds and 6 feet 6 inches (1.98 m) tall (96 kg), He was often mentioned as one of the NBA's most dangerous scorers. Jordan, who Bryant based his playing style after, has been often contrasted with Bryant. He gained much of his notoriety for making fall-away jump shots, much like Jordan. Another of Bryant's most well-known moves is what Sports Illustrated's Chris Ballard dubbed the "jab step-and pause." In this maneuver, Bryant jabs his non-pivot foot forward to make the defender relax, but instead of bringing the foot back, he pushes off of it and drives around the defender to the basket.

Bryant became known for shooting in the last seconds of close games, even when he was double- or triple-teamed, and was regarded as one of the NBA's best closers. Bryant was chosen as the player general managers would like to take a crucial shot with the game on the line in a 2012 annual poll of NBA general managers for the tenth consecutive year. Bryant delighted in playing the villain, relishing the boos before finally quieting the audience with his act. His choice of shots has also come under fire due to his aptitude for making challenging shots. Bryant endured criticism for being a high-volume, egotistical shooter during his whole career; he missed more field goal attempts in his career than any other player in NBA history. Bryant's longtime coach Phil Jackson said that Bryant had "particularly when the game isn't going his way, has a tendency to push the play. Kobe will work nonstop until his luck changes if his shot is off." "I would go 0 for 30 before I would go 0 for 9," said Bryant. "0 for 9 implies you defeated yourself, you psyched yourself out of the game."

Bryant has a stellar reputation on defense in addition to his offensive skills. When playing defense, Bryant earned few fouls, which he felt preserved his body and increased his life. Bryant received praise for his defensive performance in his latter years, although some detractors contend that this was more due to his reputation than to his actual skill.

Bryant received praise for his "Mamba mindset," or rigorous work ethic. His physique was durable over his first 17 seasons, and he had a high pain tolerance while often playing through ailments. Bryant was a strong competitor who held both his colleagues and rivals in equal contempt. Due of his high level of dedication and performance, many players have found him to be challenging to play with. Kobe was the NBA's most estranged superstar between 2004 and 2007, according to Forbes reporter Mark Heisler. He led the Lakers to two NBA titles after Shaquille O'Neal left, and during this time he became into more of a teammate's mentor than he had been earlier in his career. Phil Jackson, Bryant's former head coach, saw a significant change in Bryant's attitude toward his teammates during his two seasons as the Lakers' coach. In his early years, Bryant seldom spoke to teammates; however, he would ""embraced the team and his teammates during the latter era, contacting them while we were on the road and asking them out to dinner instead of yelling, "Give me the damn ball!" As opposed to being his own spear-carriers, the other players seemed to be his companions at this point."

BASKETBALL LEGACY

NBA Commissioner Adam Silver referred to Bryant as "one of the greatest players in the history of our game," while The New York Times described him as having "one of the most decorated careers in the history of the sport." While Sporting News and TNT both voted him their NBA player of the decade for the 2000s, Reuters referred to him as "probably the finest player of his age." He was voted the second-best shooting guard of all time, behind Michael Jordan, by ESPN in both 2008 and 2016. Bryant was referred to be his generation's Michael Jordan by players like Derrick Rose, Kevin Durant, Dirk Nowitzki, and Dwyane Wade. Bryant was referred to as "perhaps the best Laker in the history of the organization" by The Press-Enterprise. His five championships are tied for the most in team history, and he was the Lakers' all-time top scorer. The Lakers retired his career numbers 8 and 24, respectively, on December 18, 2017. Weeks after his passing, Bryant was selected as a finalist for the Naismith Memorial Basketball Hall of Fame in his first year of eligibility. He was then inducted a few months later, in April 2020. The COVID-19 epidemic forced the official entrance of the man to be postponed until 2021. Bryant was chosen to the NBA 75th Anniversary Team in October 2021, making him one of the league's all-time best players.

Bryant was regarded as one of the NBA's best all-around players, averaging 25.0 points, 5.2 rebounds, 4.7 assists, and 1.4 steals a game during his career. With 33,643 points, he is the fourth-highest scorer in league history. He was one of just four players in NBA history to have at least 25,000 points, 6,000 rebounds, and 6,000 assists in their careers. He was also the first player to have at least 30,000 points and 6,000 assists in their careers. In the 2005–06 and 2006–07 NBA seasons, Bryant ranked first in scoring.

His 81 points versus Toronto in 2006 were the second-highest in NBA history, with Chamberlain's 100 points being higher. He finished his career with at least 50 points 24 times, which ranks third in league history behind Jordan (31) and Chamberlain (118); six of those occasions, Bryant reached the 60-point mark. He averaged 40 points per month four times, making him only the third player in NBA history to do so. As the top seed in the Western Conference, Bryant led his team to the NBA Finals in 2008 and was chosen as the league's MVP that year. He received a gold medal from the American men's basketball team, often known as "The Redeem Team," in the 2008 Summer Olympics. At the 2012 Summer Olympics, he earned a another gold medal. In 2009 and 2010, he helped the Lakers win two more titles, receiving MVP of the Finals honors both times.

Bryant was an All-Star 18 times, which is second only to Kareem Abdul-total Jabbar's of 19. He was selected a record 18 times in a row, always as the starter. In the years 2003, 2011, 2013, and 2016, he received the most votes. Bryant and Bob Pettit both hold the record for most All-Star MVP awards with four each. He was named to the All-NBA Team 15 times, which ties him with Tim Duncan and Kareem Abdul-Jabbar for the most, and his 11 first team selections tie him with Karl Malone for the second-most. In addition, Bryant was chosen for the All-Defensive Team 12 times, second only to Duncan's 15 times, and the All-Defensive First Team nine times, which ties him with Jordan, Garnett, and Gary Payton for the most times in history. He was the first guard to compete in 20 NBA seasons. He was the youngest champion of the NBA Slam Dunk Contest in 1997 as well. Bryant had at least 40 points in 121 of his games during the course of his career, and 21 times he had a triple-double.

The Lakers' players donned "Black Mamba" jerseys during the 2020 NBA Playoffs as a tribute to Bryant. The black jersey, which Bryant himself designed, has a snakeskin design with yellow highlights and 16 stars to signify the team's 16 titles at the time. When the squad was wearing the "Black Mamba" jerseys in Game 2 of the Western Conference Finals victory against the Denver Nuggets, Anthony Davis hit a buzzer-beating 3-pointer and chanted Bryant's name. When questioned about the jerseys after a victory in Game 2 of the 2020 NBA Finals, LeBron James responded as follows: "Representing someone who contributed significantly to the game and the Lakers organization for more than 20 years is always an honor. Being on the ground is how we can respect him, and that's what it's all about."

A monument of Bryant and his daughter Gianna was erected near the scene of the helicopter accident on January 26, 2022, which also happened to be the second anniversary of his passing and the catastrophe. As part of the extensive makeover of the All-Star Weekend trophies in honor of the league's 75th anniversary season, the NBA updated the All-Star Game MVP trophy later in February.

ABOUT KOBE BRYANT:

LOS ANGELES LAKERS

ADJUSTING TO THE NBA (1996–1999)

In front of a packed house with standing room only, Bryant made his Summer Pro League debut in Long Beach, California, scoring 25 points. Defenders found it difficult to get in front of him, and West and Lakers coach Del Harris were impressed by his play. In four games, he averaged 24.5 points and 5.3 rebounds, including 36 points in the championship game. Bryant largely served as the backup point guard to Eddie Jones and Nick Van Exel during his first season in 1996–1997. He was the second-youngest player to ever participate in an NBA game at the time (18 years, 72 days), and he also became the league's youngest starter (18 years, 158 days). Bryant played a little amount of minutes at first, but as the season went on, he started to play more.

He played an average of 15.5 minutes each game towards the conclusion of the season. Bryant played in the Rookie Challenge during the All-Star weekend and won the 1997 Slam Dunk Contest, making history as the 18-year-old winner. Bryant was selected to the NBA All-Rookie Second Squad along with Travis Knight, another member of his bench team.

When Bryant was thrust into a leading position at the conclusion of Game 5, the Lakers defeated the Utah Jazz in the playoffs to advance to the Western Conference semifinals. Robert Horry was sent off for assaulting Jeff Hornacek of Utah, Byron Scott missed the game due to a sprained wrist, and Shaquille O'Neal fouled out with 1:46 left in the fourth quarter. The Jazz defeated the Lakers 4-1 by winning the game 98-93 in overtime despite Bryant's last four air balls.

He initially missed a two-point jump jumper that would have tied the score late in the fourth quarter before missing three three-point field goals in overtime, including two that would have won it. "Was the only man at the time who had the courage to shoot shots like that," O'Neal said.

In his second season, Bryant saw more action and started to exhibit more of his skills as a gifted young guard. Bryant's scoring average increased from 7.6 to 15.4 points per game as a consequence. When the Lakers "played small," Bryant would get more playing time because he would play small forward with the guards he typically backed up. Bryant was the NBA's Sixth Man of the Year runner-up, and because to fan vote, he also became the league's youngest-ever starter for an All-Star game. It was the first time since 1983 that four members of the same team were chosen to participate in the same All-Star Game when he was joined by teammates O'Neal, Van Exel, and Jones. Bryant averaged 15.4 points per game throughout the season, the most of any non-starter.

Bryant made a name for himself in the league as a top guard during the 1998–99 season. Bryant played every game during the 50-game lockout-shortened season because starter guards Van Exel and Jones had been moved. Bryant agreed to a six-year, $70 million contract extension for the current campaign. He remained with the Lakers as a result until the 2003–04 campaign. Sports journalists were comparing his abilities to those of Magic Johnson and Michael Jordan even at the beginning of his career. However, the postseason outcomes weren't much better, as the Lakers lost to the San Antonio Spurs in straight games in the Western Conference Semifinals.

THREE-PEAT (1999–2002)

Bryant's situation would become better once Phil Jackson became the Lakers' head coach in 1999. After years of consistent development, Bryant emerged as one of the league's top shooting guards, earning spots on the All-NBA, All-Star, and All-Defensive teams. Bryant and O'Neal's center-guard combo helped the Lakers become title contenders. Jackson used the triangle approach he developed to help the Chicago Bulls win six championships; this offense helped Bryant and O'Neal go to the NBA's top echelon. The successive victories of three championships in 2000, 2001, and 2002 added credence to this opinion.

Due to a hand injury sustained during a preseason game against the Washington Wizards, Bryant missed the first six weeks of the 1999–2000 season. During the 1999–2000 season, Bryant's performance increased in every statistical category after he returned and began playing more than 38 minutes per game. This includes leading the club in game-by-game assists and steals. The Lakers won 67 games, which is tied for the fifth-most in NBA history thanks to the combination of O'Neal and Bryant with a potent bench. O'Neal won the MVP award after that, while Bryant received his first career selections to the All-NBA Second Team and All-NBA Defensive Team (the youngest player to receive All-Defensive honors). Bryant had several big postseason games despite being O'Neal's understudy, including a 25-point, 11-rebound, 7-assist, 4-block effort against Portland Trail Blazers in Game 7 of the Western Conference Finals. In order to win the game and the series, he also threw an alley-oop pass to O'Neal. Bryant suffered an ankle injury in Game 2 of the 2000 Finals against the Indiana Pacers in the second quarter as he landed on Jalen Rose's foot. Rose then said he deliberately put his foot beneath Bryant. Bryant's injury prevented him from returning to the game, and he missed Game 3 as well. In Game 4, Bryant led the club to an overtime win after O'Neal fouled out of the contest by scoring 22 points in the second half. Bryant made the game-winning jumper to give the Lakers a 120–118 advantage. The Lakers won their first title since 1988 by winning Game 6 116-111.

Bryant performed similarly to the previous season statistically in 2000–01, but he averaged six more points per game (28.5). Additionally, that year saw the start of disputes between Bryant and O'Neal. Bryant continued to lead the club in assists, averaging five per game. However, the Lakers only managed to win 56 games, an 11-game decline from the previous season. In response, the Lakers went 15-1 in the postseason. In the first round, they handily defeated the Portland Trail Blazers. The Lakers defeated the Sacramento Kings in straight games in the playoffs. Bryant had a series-clinching 48 points, 16 rebounds, and 3 assists in Game 4 against the Kings. They won the Conference Finals series against San Antonio Spurs 3-0 to proceed to the Finals, where they lost their first game in overtime to the Philadelphia 76ers. They would go on to win the next four games and deliver Los Angeles their second title in as many years. Bryant played a lot of minutes throughout the playoffs, increasing his per-game averages to 29.4 points, 7.3 rebounds, and 6.1 assists. Bryant was named the league's top player during the playoffs, according to teammate O'Neal. In the end, Bryant was selected for the second consecutive year to the All-NBA Second Team and All-NBA Defensive Team. He also received votes to start the NBA All-Star Game for a third consecutive year (no game in 1999).

Bryant played 80 games for the first time in his career in the 2001–02 season. Bryant scored a then-career-high 56 points, along with five rebounds and four assists, on January 14, 2002, as the visiting Memphis Grizzlies were defeated 120–81. Averaging 25.2 points, 5.5 rebounds, and 5.5 assists per game, he maintained his all-around performance. Bryant once again led his team in assists while shooting at a career-high 46.9 percent.

After scoring 31 points in Philadelphia, where he was booed heavily by the crowd throughout the game due to his previous statement to a 76ers heckler during the Finals that the Lakers were "about to tear your hearts out," he won his first All-Star MVP award. Bryant was selected to the All-NBA First Team for the first time in his career in addition to being chosen to the All-NBA Defensive Team once again. In that season, the Lakers won 58 games and finished behind their cross-state rival Sacramento Kings in the Pacific Division standings. Following the Lakers' March 1, 2002 victory against the Indiana Pacers, Bryant hit Reggie Miller of the Pacers, earning him a one-game suspension.

Compared to the Lakers' record-breaking run the year before, the journey to the Finals would prove to be much more difficult. In the first two rounds of the playoffs, the Lakers swept the Blazers and beat the Spurs 4-1, but they did not enjoy a home-court advantage against the Sacramento Kings. This was the first time the Lakers have faced a seven-game series since the 2000 Western Conference Finals. The Lakers, though, were able to defeat their division rivals and go to their third straight NBA Finals. Bryant scored 26.8 points, 51.4 percent shooting, 5.8 rebounds, and 5.3 assists per game in the 2002 Finals against the New Jersey Nets. He also contributed 25 percent of the team's points to the scoreboard. Bryant became the youngest player to win three titles when he was 23 years old. Bryant's performance in the fourth quarter of games, particularly the last two rounds of the playoffs, was noteworthy and highly applauded. Bryant's status as a "clutch player" was solidified by this.

COMING UP SHORT (2002–2004)

In an 87-82 defeat to the visiting Spurs in the opening game of the 2002–03 season, Bryant finished with 27 points, 10 rebounds, 5 assists, and 4 steals. In a 108-93 victory against the LA Clippers on November 1, Bryant had a triple-double of 33 points, 15 rebounds, and 12 assists. On January 7, 2003, he also broke the previous NBA record most three-pointers made in a single game when he hit 12 against the Seattle SuperSonics. Bryant scored 40 or more points in nine straight games while averaging 40.6 points for the whole month of February. He also averaged 30 points a game and went on a historic run. He also had career-high averages of 6.9 rebounds, 5.9 assists, and 2.2 steals per game. Bryant finished third in the voting for the MVP award and was once again selected to the All-NBA and All-Defensive First Teams. The Lakers struggled in the postseason after going 50-32 during the regular season, falling to the eventual NBA champion San Antonio Spurs in the Western Conference semi-finals in six games.

In order to make another run at the NBA title the following year, the Lakers were able to acquire NBA All-Stars Karl Malone and Gary Payton. Prior to the start of the season, Bryant was detained for sexual assault. In order to attend court earlier in the day and fly to play games later that day, Bryant was forced to skip several games. The Lakers faced the Portland Trail Blazers in the last game of the regular season. In order to win the match and the Pacific Division, Bryant hit two buzzer-beating shots. With 1.1 seconds remaining in the fourth quarter, Bryant scored a three-pointer to end the game and force overtime. After the game entered its second overtime, Bryant hit another three-pointer with seconds left to help the Lakers defeat the Blazers, 105-104.

The Lakers were able to make it to the NBA Finals because to a starting group that included O'Neal, Malone, Payton, and Bryant. The Detroit Pistons, who won their first championship since 1990, stunned them in a series of five games. Bryant averaged 22.6 points per game, 4.4 assists, and 35.1 field goal percentage in the series. Jackson's coaching agreement was not extended, and Rudy Tomjanovich was named in his place. In exchange for Lamar Odom, Caron Butler, and Brian Grant, O'Neal was dealt to the Miami Heat. The next day, Bryant re-signed with the Lakers on a seven-year, $136.4 million deal after turning down a six-year, $100 million offer to join the Los Angeles Clippers.

SCORING RECORDS AND PLAYOFF UPSETS (2004-2007)

Due to all that had transpired the previous year, Bryant's image had been severely tarnished and he was the target of intense scrutiny and criticism throughout the 2004–05 season. The Last Season: A Team in Search of Its Soul, which Jackson penned, was a particularly destructive volley. The book included various critiques of Bryant and documented the events of the Lakers' turbulent 2003–04 season. Jackson referred to Bryant as "un-coachable" in the book. Tomjanovich abruptly left his position as Lakers coach in the middle of the season, claiming reoccurring health issues and tiredness. Without Tomjanovich, longtime assistant coach Frank Hamblen was left in charge of the Lakers' remaining regular season games. At 27.6 points per game, Bryant was the second-highest scorer in the league, but the Lakers finished 34-48 and missed the playoffs for the first time in more than ten years due to a lackluster supporting cast. Bryant's overall standing in the NBA declined throughout the year as he was both dropped to the All-NBA Third Team and did not make the NBA All-Defensive Team. Bryant fought publicly with Malone and Ray Allen throughout the season.

The 2005–06 basketball season was a turning point in Bryant's career. Jackson came back to lead the Lakers despite prior hostilities with Bryant. The move was supported by Bryant, and it seems that the two men got along well the second time around and led the Lakers back into the playoffs. Bryant's best statistical season of his career was the product of his individual scoring achievements. Against the Dallas Mavericks on December 20, 2005, Bryant scored 62 points in three quarters. Bryant outscored the whole Mavericks team 62-61 heading into the fourth quarter, which is the first time a player has accomplished this through three quarters since the shot clock was introduced.

On January 16, 2006, when the Lakers played the Miami Heat, Bryant and Shaquille O'Neal made headlines by shaking hands and hugging before to the game, signaling an end to the animosity that had festered between them. The two were spotted laughing together at the 2006 NBA All-Star Game one month later.

Bryant had a career-high 81 points on January 22, 2006, as the Los Angeles Lakers defeated the Toronto Raptors 122-104. Bryant's 81-point performance eclipsed Elgin Baylor's 71-point club record and was the second-highest point total in NBA history, after only Chamberlain's 100-point performance in 1962. In contrast to Chamberlain, who received many feeds from teammates for inside baskets during a rout victory, Bryant generated most of his own shots, primarily from outside, during a game in which the Lakers trailed by 14 points at halftime and did not take control until the fourth quarter. In Philadelphia's 169-147 victory, Chamberlain scored 59 percent of his team's points, compared to Bryant's 66 percent for the 122 points scored by the Lakers. Chamberlain was playing in an age when games were played at a quicker tempo and scoring chances were more common. Bryant joined Chamberlain and Baylor as the only players to have scored 45 points or more in four straight games in the same month, becoming the first player to do it since 1964. Bryant averaged 43.4 points per game in January, which is the eighth-highest single-month scoring average in NBA history and the most of any player outside Chamberlain. Bryant established Lakers single-season club marks for the most 40-point games (27) and the most points scored by the conclusion of the 2005–06 campaign (2,832). He became only the fifth player in league history to average at least 35 points per game in a season, winning the scoring championship for the first time. He did this by scoring 35.4 points per game on average. In the voting for the 2006 NBA Most Valuable Player Award, Bryant came in fourth place but garnered 22 first-place votes, second only to winner Steve Nash. Later in the year, it was revealed that Bryant will switch from wearing the number 8 to the number 24 for the beginning of the 2006–07 campaign. Bryant's original high school identifier was 24, and he later changed it to 33.

Bryant said on TNT after the Lakers' season concluded that he wanted number 24 as a rookie but couldn't have it since it was worn by George McCloud and number 33 was retired with Kareem Abdul-Jabbar. At the Adidas ABCD camp, Bryant wore 143, thus he added those numbers to arrive at 8. The Lakers defeated the Phoenix Suns in the first round of the playoffs, taking a 3-1 series lead thanks to Bryant's overtime-instigating and game-winning shots in Game 4. In Game 6, they came within six seconds of defeating the second-seeded Suns, but they ultimately fell short, falling 126-118 in overtime. Bryant averaged 27.9 points per game throughout the series, but the Lakers eventually faltered and lost to the Suns in seven games. Bryant was chastised for only taking three shots in the second half of the 121-90 Game 7 defeat to Phoenix after scoring 50 points on 20 of 35 attempts in the Game 6 loss.

Bryant was chosen to play in his tenth All-Star Game during the 2006–07 season, and on February 18, he had 31 points, 6 assists, and 6 steals to win his second All-Star Game MVP award of his career. Bryant got engaged in a number of on-court confrontations during the course of the season. He flailed his arm on January 28 in an effort to generate contact on a possible game-winning jump jumper, elbowing San Antonio Spurs player Manu Ginóbili in the face. Bryant was benched for the next Madison Square Garden matchup against the New York Knicks after a league investigation. Bryant was suspended on the grounds that he had made a "unnatural gesture" by swinging his arm backward. He seemed to repeat the gesture again, on March 6, hitting Minnesota Timberwolves player Marko Jari. Bryant received his second one-game ban from the NBA on March 7. He elbowed Kyle Korver in the face in his first game back on March 9, which was subsequently reclassified as a Type 1 egregious foul. Bryant broke the Lakers' seven-game losing run on March 16 by tallying a season-high 65 points in a home game against the Portland Trail Blazers. The second-best scoring effort of his 11-year career was this one. Bryant became the second Laker to score three consecutive 50-plus point games, a milestone previously accomplished by Jordan in 1987, when he scored 50 points against the Minnesota Timberwolves.

He then followed it up with 60 points in a victory over the Memphis Grizzlies on the road. Baylor was the only other Laker to accomplish this feat; in December 1962, he also reached 50+ points in three straight games. After Chamberlain, who accomplished it twice with streaks of five and seven games, Bryant became the second player in NBA history to have four consecutive 50-point games the next day, in a game against the New Orleans/Oklahoma City Hornets. Only Chamberlain had more 50-plus point games than Bryant did at the end of the season. That year, Bryant also won his second consecutive scoring crown. His jersey rose to the #1 spot among NBA jerseys sold in China and the United States during the 2006–07 season. Many media members have credited Bryant's new jersey number and his ongoing All-Star play on the court for the increased sales. The Lakers were once again defeated 4-1 by the Phoenix Suns in the first round of the NBA playoffs in 2007. Due to all that had transpired the previous year, Bryant's image had been severely tarnished and he was the target of intense scrutiny and criticism throughout the 2004–05 season.

The Last Season: A Team in Search of Its Soul, which Jackson penned, was a particularly destructive volley. The book included various critiques of Bryant and documented the events of the Lakers' turbulent 2003–04 season. Jackson referred to Bryant as "un-coachable" in the book. Tomjanovich abruptly left his position as Lakers coach in the middle of the season, claiming reoccurring health issues and tiredness. Without Tomjanovich, longtime assistant coach Frank Hamblen was left in charge of the Lakers' remaining regular season games. At 27.6 points per game, Bryant was the second-highest scorer in the league, but the Lakers finished 34-48 and missed the playoffs for the first time in more than ten years due to a lackluster supporting cast. Bryant's overall standing in the NBA declined throughout the year as he was both dropped to the All-NBA Third Team and did not make the NBA All-Defensive Team. Bryant fought publicly with Malone and Ray Allen throughout the season.

The 2005–06 basketball season was a turning point in Bryant's career. Jackson came back to lead the Lakers despite prior hostilities with Bryant. The move was supported by Bryant, and it seems that the two men got along well the second time around and led the Lakers back into the playoffs. Bryant's best statistical season of his career was the product of his individual scoring achievements. Against the Dallas Mavericks on December 20, 2005, Bryant scored 62 points in three quarters. Bryant outscored the whole Mavericks team 62-61 heading into the fourth quarter, which is the first time a player has accomplished this through three quarters since the shot clock was introduced. On January 16, 2006, when the Lakers played the Miami Heat, Bryant and Shaquille O'Neal made headlines by shaking hands and hugging before to the game, signaling an end to the animosity that had festered between them. The two were spotted laughing together at the 2006 NBA All-Star Game one month later.

Bryant had a career-high 81 points on January 22, 2006, as the Los Angeles Lakers defeated the Toronto Raptors 122-104. Bryant's 81-point performance eclipsed Elgin Baylor's 71-point club record and was the second-highest point total in NBA history, after only Chamberlain's 100-point performance in 1962. In contrast to Chamberlain, who received many feeds from teammates for inside baskets during a rout victory, Bryant generated most of his own shots, primarily from outside, during a game in which the Lakers trailed by 14 points at halftime and did not take control until the fourth quarter. In Philadelphia's 169-147 victory, Chamberlain scored 59 percent of his team's points, compared to Bryant's 66 percent for the 122 points scored by the Lakers. Chamberlain was playing in an age when games were played at a quicker tempo and scoring chances were more common. Bryant joined Chamberlain and Baylor as the only players to have scored 45 points or more in four straight games in the same month, becoming the first player to do it since 1964.

Bryant averaged 43.4 points per game in January, which is the eighth-highest single-month scoring average in NBA history and the most of any player outside Chamberlain. Bryant established Lakers single-season club marks for the most 40-point games (27) and the most points scored by the conclusion of the 2005–06 campaign (2,832). He became only the fifth player in league history to average at least 35 points per game in a season, winning the scoring championship for the first time. He did this by scoring 35.4 points per game on average. In the voting for the 2006 NBA Most Valuable Player Award, Bryant came in fourth place but garnered 22 first-place votes, second only to winner Steve Nash.

Later in the year, it was revealed that Bryant will switch from wearing the number 8 to the number 24 for the beginning of the 2006–07 campaign. Bryant's original high school identifier was 24, and he later changed it to 33. Bryant said on TNT after the Lakers' season concluded that he wanted number 24 as a rookie but couldn't have it since it was worn by George McCloud and number 33 was retired with Kareem Abdul-Jabbar. At the Adidas ABCD camp, Bryant wore 143, thus he added those numbers to arrive at 8. The Lakers defeated the Phoenix Suns in the first round of the playoffs, taking a 3-1 series lead thanks to Bryant's overtime-instigating and game-winning shots in Game 4. In Game 6, they came within six seconds of defeating the second-seeded Suns, but they ultimately fell short, falling 126-118 in overtime. Bryant averaged 27.9 points per game throughout the series, but the Lakers eventually faltered and lost to the Suns in seven games. Bryant was chastised for only taking three shots in the second half of the 121-90 Game 7 defeat to Phoenix after scoring 50 points on 20 of 35 attempts in the Game 6 loss. Bryant was chosen to play in his tenth All-Star Game during the 2006–07 season, and on February 18, he had 31 points, 6 assists, and 6 steals to win his second All-Star Game MVP award of his career. Bryant got engaged in a number of on-court confrontations during the course of the season.

He flailed his arm on January 28 in an effort to generate contact on a possible game-winning jump jumper, elbowing San Antonio Spurs player Manu Ginóbili in the face. Bryant was benched for the next Madison Square Garden matchup against the New York Knicks after a league investigation. Bryant was suspended on the grounds that he had made a "unnatural gesture" by swinging his arm backward. He seemed to repeat the gesture again, on March 6, hitting Minnesota Timberwolves player Marko Jari. Bryant received his second one-game ban from the NBA on March 7. He elbowed Kyle Korver in the face in his first game back on March 9, which was subsequently reclassified as a Type 1 egregious foul.

Bryant broke the Lakers' seven-game losing run on March 16 by tallying a season-high 65 points in a home game against the Portland Trail Blazers. The second-best scoring effort of his 11-year career was this one. Bryant became the second Laker to score three consecutive 50-plus point games, a milestone previously accomplished by Jordan in 1987, when he scored 50 points against the Minnesota Timberwolves. He then followed it up with 60 points in a victory over the Memphis Grizzlies on the road. Baylor was the only other Laker to accomplish this feat; in December 1962, he also reached 50+ points in three straight games. After Chamberlain, who accomplished it twice with streaks of five and seven games, Bryant became the second player in NBA history to have four consecutive 50-point games the next day, in a game against the New Orleans/Oklahoma City Hornets. Only Chamberlain had more 50-plus point games than Bryant did at the end of the season. That year, Bryant also won his second consecutive scoring crown. His jersey rose to the #1 spot among NBA jerseys sold in China and the United States during the 2006–07 season. Many media members have credited Bryant's new jersey number and his ongoing All-Star play on the court for the increased sales. The Lakers were once again defeated 4-1 by the Phoenix Suns in the first round of the NBA playoffs in 2007.

BACK ON TOP (2007-2010)

Bryant reportedly requested to be transferred on May 27, 2007, according to a source from ESPN, if Jerry West did not rejoin the organization with full control. Later, Bryant expressed his wish for West to rejoin the team, but he refrained from saying that he would prefer to be moved if that didn't happen. Three days later, however, Bryant publicly said, "I want to be transferred," in response to a Lakers "insider" who had implied that Bryant was to blame for Shaquille O'Neal's departure from the franchise. Three hours after making that declaration, Bryant said in a different interview that he had changed his mind and withdrawn his desire for a trade after speaking with head coach Jackson. Later, in a notorious homemade film, Bryant was heard arguing that center Andrew Bynum ought to have been swapped for All-Star Jason Kidd.

In a game against the New York Knicks on December 23, 2007, Bryant scored 39 points to go along with 11 rebounds and 8 assists to become the youngest player (29 years, 122 days) to achieve 20,000 points. LeBron James has subsequently shattered this record. In a defeat against the Memphis Grizzlies on March 28, Bryant produced a season-high 53 points along with 10 rebounds.

Bryant played all 82 regular-season games without having surgery despite suffering an injury to his shooting hand's little finger on February 5, 2008, which was characterized as "a complete rupture of the radial collateral ligament, an avulsion fracture, and a volar plate damage at the MCP joint." In relation to his ailment, he said, "Any surgery should wait until after the Lakers season and the summer Olympics, in my opinion. But this is a wound that I, along with the Lakers' medical team, will simply have to keep tracking day by day."

Bryant guided his club to a West-leading 57-25 record with the help of the deal for All-Star Pau Gasol. Bryant was formally named the league MVP on May 6, 2008, after the Lakers swept the Nuggets in the first round. He stated: "The journey was really lengthy. I'm really honored to represent this company and this city." Bryant accepted his MVP award from NBA commissioner David Stern at the news conference while West, who was in charge of luring Bryant to the Lakers, was there. Stern declared: "Kobe was due it. He's just had another fantastic season. I'm not surprised in the least." Bryant was selected to the All-NBA team for the third consecutive year and a career-high six times on May 8, 2008, in addition to taking home the MVP title. Together with Kevin Garnett, he would later top the NBA All-Defensive First Team, garnering 52 points total, including 24 first-place honors and his ninth nomination.

The Lakers finished the 2007–08 regular season with a 57–25 record, taking first place in the Western Conference and securing a matchup against the Nuggets in the first round. In Game 1, Bryant scored 18 of his 32 points in the last eight minutes to put Los Angeles comfortably ahead. Bryant said he played the majority of the game as a decoy. Denver became the first 50-win club to be eliminated in the first round of the playoffs since the Memphis Grizzlies were defeated by the San Antonio Spurs in four games in 2004 as a result. Bryant scored 38 points as the Lakers defeated the Jazz in Game 1 of the subsequent round against them. Even though Bryant averaged 33.5 points per game, the Lakers lost Games 3 and 4. They also won the next game. Later, the Lakers won the next two games to go to the semifinals. This qualified them to face the San Antonio Spurs in the Western Conference Finals. The Lakers eliminated the Spurs in five games, advancing to play the Boston Celtics in the NBA Finals. This was the seventh NBA Finals appearance of Bryant's career and the first sans O'Neal. The Boston Celtics eventually defeated the Lakers in six games.

Bryant chose not to undergo surgery to fix his right pinkie in the first few days of September 2008. The Lakers started the 2008-09 season well, winning their first seven games. By going 17-2 to open the season and 21-3 by the middle of December, Bryant had helped the squad equal the franchise record most victories. He was chosen to play in his 11th straight All-Star Game as a starter, and in addition to being voted Western Conference Player of the Week three times, he was also awarded Western Conference Player of the Month for the months of December and January. Bryant established a Madison Square Garden record for most points scored when he scored 61 in a game against the Knicks on February 2, 2009. Bryant finished with 27 points, 4 assists, 4 rebounds, and 4 steals at the 2009 NBA All-Star Game. He shared the MVP honors with his old colleague O'Neal. The Lakers had the best record in the West at the end of the regular season (65-17). In addition to being named to the All-NBA First Team and All-Defensive First Team for the eighth season in his career, Bryant finished second in the MVP vote behind James.

The Lakers won the first two rounds of the playoffs against the Utah Jazz in five games and the Houston Rockets in seven games. The Los Angeles Lakers secured their second consecutive trip to the NBA Finals by defeating the Denver Nuggets in the Conference Finals in six games. In five games, the Lakers beat the Orlando Magic. After winning his fourth title, Bryant received his first NBA Finals MVP trophy for averaging 32.4 points, 7.4 assists, 5.6 rebounds, 1.4 steals, and 1.4 blocks per game. He became the first player to average at least 32.4 points and 7.4 assists for a Finals series since West in the NBA Finals of 1969, as well as the first since Jordan to average 30 points, 5 rebounds, and 5 assists for a team that won the championship. Between the 1999–2000 and 2008–09 seasons, Bryant scored 21,065 points in regular season action to lead the league as its top scorer.

Bryant scored six game-winning shots in the 2009–10 season, including a buzzer-beating, one-legged 3-pointer on December 4, 2009, against the Miami Heat. The shot, in Bryant's opinion, was "one of the luckiest he has ever made." Bryant broke his right index finger in an avulsion fracture a week later while playing against the Minnesota Timberwolves. Bryant decided to play through the ailment rather than taking any time off to heal it. Five days after suffering a finger injury, he scored another game-winning shot, this time in overtime against the Milwaukee Bucks after missing a chance in regulation. Bryant surpassed Chamberlain to become the player with 25,000 career points at the age of 31, 151 days, during the season. He proceeded to make clutch shots against the Sacramento Kings and the Boston Celtics, nailing another game-winning three-pointer and what would ultimately be the game-winning field goal. He overtook West the next day to take over as the Lakers franchise's all-time top scorer. Bryant, who had missed the previous five games due to an ankle injury, returned against the Memphis Grizzlies with four seconds left in the game, giving the Los Angeles Lakers a one-point lead. Two weeks later, he defeated the Toronto Raptors with his sixth season-winning shot.

Bryant agreed to a three-year, $87 million contract extension on April 2, 2010. Due to finger and knee ailments, Bryant missed four of the last five games of the regular season. Bryant missed nine games as a consequence of his many ailments during the season. The Lakers faced the Oklahoma City Thunder at the start of the postseason as the top seed in the Western Conference, and ultimately won in six games. The Lakers progressed to the Western Conference Finals, where they played the Phoenix Suns, after sweeping the Utah Jazz in the second round. With his 13 assists in Game 2, Bryant established a new postseason record and gave the Laker team its most assists in the playoffs since Magic Johnson had 13 in 1996. The Lakers eventually won the series in six games, claiming the Western Conference Championship and making a third consecutive trip to the NBA Finals. In a rematch against the Boston Celtics, who won the 2008 title,

Bryant led the Lakers back from a 13-point third-quarter deficit to win the championship despite shooting 6 for 24 from the floor. He scored 10 of his game-high 23 points in the fourth quarter and ended with 15 rebounds. Bryant won his fifth title and was named the NBA Finals MVP for the second time in a row. The Los Angeles Lakers defeated the Boston Celtics in Game 7 of the NBA Finals for the first time ever. Of all of his five titles, Bryant said that this one gave him the greatest satisfaction. Bryant reportedly requested to be transferred on May 27, 2007, according to a source from ESPN, if Jerry West did not rejoin the organization with full control. Later, Bryant expressed his wish for West to rejoin the team, but he refrained from saying that he would prefer to be moved if that didn't happen. Three days later, however, Bryant publicly said, "I want to be transferred," in response to a Lakers "insider" who had implied that Bryant was to blame for Shaquille O'Neal's departure from the franchise. Three hours after making that declaration, Bryant said in a different interview that he had changed his mind and withdrawn his desire for a trade after speaking with head coach Jackson. Later, in a notorious homemade film, Bryant was heard arguing that center Andrew Bynum ought to have been swapped for All-Star Jason Kidd.

In a game against the New York Knicks on December 23, 2007, Bryant scored 39 points to go along with 11 rebounds and 8 assists to become the youngest player (29 years, 122 days) to achieve 20,000 points. LeBron James has subsequently shattered this record. In a defeat against the Memphis Grizzlies on March 28, Bryant produced a season-high 53 points along with 10 rebounds.

Bryant played all 82 regular-season games without having surgery despite suffering an injury to his shooting hand's little finger on February 5, 2008, which was characterized as "a complete rupture of the radial collateral ligament, an avulsion fracture, and a volar plate damage at the MCP joint." In relation to his ailment, he said, "Any surgery should wait until after the Lakers season and the summer Olympics, in my opinion. But this is a wound that I, along with the Lakers' medical team, will simply have to keep tracking day by day."

Bryant guided his club to a West-leading 57-25 record with the help of the deal for All-Star Pau Gasol. Bryant was formally named the league MVP on May 6, 2008, after the Lakers swept the Nuggets in the first round. He stated: "The journey was really lengthy. I'm really honored to represent this company and this city." Bryant accepted his MVP award from NBA commissioner David Stern at the news conference while West, who was in charge of luring Bryant to the Lakers, was there. Stern declared: "Kobe was due it. He's just had another fantastic season. I'm not surprised in the least." Bryant was selected to the All-NBA team for the third consecutive year and a career-high six times on May 8, 2008, in addition to taking home the MVP title. Together with Kevin Garnett, he would later top the NBA All-Defensive First Team, garnering 52 points total, including 24 first-place honors and his ninth nomination.

The Lakers finished the 2007–08 regular season with a 57–25 record, taking first place in the Western Conference and securing a matchup against the Nuggets in the first round. In Game 1, Bryant scored 18 of his 32 points in the last eight minutes to put Los Angeles comfortably ahead. Bryant said he played the majority of the game as a decoy. Denver became the first 50-win club to be eliminated in the first round of the playoffs since the Memphis Grizzlies were defeated by the San Antonio Spurs in four games in 2004 as a result. Bryant scored 38 points as the Lakers defeated the Jazz in Game 1 of the subsequent round against them. Even though Bryant averaged 33.5 points per game, the Lakers lost Games 3 and 4. They also won the next game. Later, the Lakers won the next two games to go to the semifinals. This qualified them to face the San Antonio Spurs in the Western Conference Finals. The Lakers eliminated the Spurs in five games, advancing to play the Boston Celtics in the NBA Finals. This was the seventh NBA Finals appearance of Bryant's career and the first sans O'Neal. The Boston Celtics eventually defeated the Lakers in six games.

Bryant chose not to undergo surgery to fix his right pinkie in the first few days of September 2008. The Lakers started the 2008-09 season well, winning their first seven games.

By going 17-2 to open the season and 21-3 by the middle of December, Bryant had helped the squad equal the franchise record most victories. He was chosen to play in his 11th straight All-Star Game as a starter, and in addition to being voted Western Conference Player of the Week three times, he was also awarded Western Conference Player of the Month for the months of December and January. Bryant established a Madison Square Garden record for most points scored when he scored 61 in a game against the Knicks on February 2, 2009. Bryant finished with 27 points, 4 assists, 4 rebounds, and 4 steals at the 2009 NBA All-Star Game. He shared the MVP honors with his old colleague O'Neal. The Lakers had the best record in the West at the end of the regular season (65-17). In addition to being named to the All-NBA First Team and All-Defensive First Team for the eighth season in his career, Bryant finished second in the MVP vote behind James.

The Lakers won the first two rounds of the playoffs against the Utah Jazz in five games and the Houston Rockets in seven games. The Los Angeles Lakers secured their second consecutive trip to the NBA Finals by defeating the Denver Nuggets in the Conference Finals in six games. In five games, the Lakers beat the Orlando Magic. After winning his fourth title, Bryant received his first NBA Finals MVP trophy for averaging 32.4 points, 7.4 assists, 5.6 rebounds, 1.4 steals, and 1.4 blocks per game. He became the first player to average at least 32.4 points and 7.4 assists for a Finals series since West in the NBA Finals of 1969, as well as the first since Jordan to average 30 points, 5 rebounds, and 5 assists for a team that won the championship. Between the 1999–2000 and 2008–09 seasons, Bryant scored 21,065 points in regular season action to lead the league as its top scorer.

Bryant scored six game-winning shots in the 2009–10 season, including a buzzer-beating, one-legged 3-pointer on December 4, 2009, against the Miami Heat. The shot, in Bryant's opinion, was "one of the luckiest he has ever made." Bryant broke his right index finger in an avulsion fracture a week later while playing against the Minnesota Timberwolves.

Bryant decided to play through the ailment rather than taking any time off to heal it. Five days after suffering a finger injury, he scored another game-winning shot, this time in overtime against the Milwaukee Bucks after missing a chance in regulation. Bryant surpassed Chamberlain to become the player with 25,000 career points at the age of 31, 151 days, during the season. He proceeded to make clutch shots against the Sacramento Kings and the Boston Celtics, nailing another game-winning three-pointer and what would ultimately be the game-winning field goal. He overtook West the next day to take over as the Lakers franchise's all-time top scorer. Bryant, who had missed the previous five games due to an ankle injury, returned against the Memphis Grizzlies with four seconds left in the game, giving the Los Angeles Lakers a one-point lead. Two weeks later, he defeated the Toronto Raptors with his sixth season-winning shot.

Bryant agreed to a three-year, $87 million contract extension on April 2, 2010. Due to finger and knee ailments, Bryant missed four of the last five games of the regular season. Bryant missed nine games as a consequence of his many ailments during the season. The Lakers faced the Oklahoma City Thunder at the start of the postseason as the top seed in the Western Conference, and ultimately won in six games. The Lakers progressed to the Western Conference Finals, where they played the Phoenix Suns, after sweeping the Utah Jazz in the second round. With his 13 assists in Game 2, Bryant established a new postseason record and gave the Laker team its most assists in the playoffs since Magic Johnson had 13 in 1996. The Lakers eventually won the series in six games, claiming the Western Conference Championship and making a third consecutive trip to the NBA Finals. In a rematch against the Boston Celtics, who won the 2008 title, Bryant led the Lakers back from a 13-point third-quarter deficit to win the championship despite shooting 6 for 24 from the floor. He scored 10 of his game-high 23 points in the fourth quarter and ended with 15 rebounds. Bryant won his fifth title and was named the NBA Finals MVP for the second time in a row. The Los Angeles Lakers defeated the Boston Celtics in Game 7 of the NBA Finals for the first time ever. Of all of his five titles, Bryant said that this one gave him the greatest satisfaction.

CHASING A SIXTH CHAMPIONSHIP (2010–2013)

To equal Jordan's total of championships, Bryant want a sixth. The Lakers won their first eight games of the 2010–11 season. Bryant reached 26,000 career points in his ninth game of the year against the Denver Nuggets, becoming him the youngest player in NBA history to do so. Bryant also accomplished a triple-double for the first time since January 21, 2009. He scored 27,000 points on January 30 against the Celtics, becoming him the youngest player to do so. Bryant joined the exclusive group of seven players on February 1, 2011, who each have at least 25,000 points, 5,000 rebounds, and 5,000 assists. On February 10, the Lakers defeated the Celtics 92-86 in Boston after coming back from an early 15-point hole thanks in large part to Bryant, who tallied 20 of his 23 points in the second half.

The Lakers entered the game with a 0-5 record and an average loss of 11 points per game; it was their first win of the season against one of the top four teams in the league. Bryant, who received the most votes and was chosen to play in his 13th consecutive All-Star game, scored 37 points, 14 rebounds, three steals, and earned his fourth All-Star MVP title in 2011. He now has the same number of All-Star MVP trophies as Hall of Famer Bob Pettit. Bryant passed John Havlicek, Dominique Wilkins, Oscar Robertson, Hakeem Olajuwon, Elvin Hayes, and Moses Malone to move up to sixth place on the NBA's all-time scoring record during the current season. Bryant's season-ending average of less than 20 shots per game was his lowest since the 2003–04 campaign.

Bryant received a $100,000 fine from the NBA on April 13, 2011, for yelling a homophobic epithet at referee Bennie Adams during the game the day before. Bryant's rhetoric was described as "disgraceful" and "distasteful" by the Human Rights Campaign, while the Gay & Lesbian Alliance Against Defamation applauded the NBA's decision to punish Bryant. Bryant said he intended to appeal his punishment and was willing to talk to LGBT rights organizations about the situation. Later, he expressed regret for using the slur. Bryant and other Lakers were featured in a Lakers PSA criticizing his actions. When they were defeated by the Dallas Mavericks in the second round of the playoffs, the team's attempt at a third consecutive championship came to an end.

In order to cure the discomfort in his left knee and ankle, Bryant underwent an experimental platelet-rich plasma treatment called Orthokine in Germany. In the off-season, Mike Brown succeeded the departed Jackson as head coach of the Lakers. Bryant played through a wrist injury to start the season. Bryant scored 48 points against the Suns on January 10, 2012. In reference to a preseason ESPN list of the NBA's top players, Bryant said, "Not bad for the seventh-best player in the league." In his subsequent three games, he scored 40, 42, and 42 points. Only Chamberlain has more times in his career (six) to have scored 40 or more points in four successive games (19 times). Bryant overtook Jordan as the NBA All-Star Game's all-time leading scorer with 27 points in the 2012 NBA All-Star Game. Following a tough foul by Dwyane Wade in the third quarter of the All-Star Game, he also sustained a fractured nose and a concussion. Bryant missed seven games in April due to an injured left shin. Three games before the regular season's finish, he came back. After needing 38 points to overcome Kevin Durant, he chose to sit out the season's last game against Sacramento rather than pursue a third scoring championship in the NBA. In what would be Bryant's last playoff participation, the Lakers were eliminated from the playoffs by Durant and Oklahoma City in the second round. The loss came in five games.

In 2012–13, the Lakers acquired Steve Nash, a point guard, and center Dwight Howard. Bryant overtook Magic Johnson (1,724) as the Lakers' all-time thefts leader on November 2, 2012, when he scored 40 points and had two steals. For the first time in 34 years and only the fourth time in team history, the Lakers opened the season 0-3 after losing to the Clippers. Coach Brown was let go after his team went 1-4 to open the year. Mike D'Antoni, who Bryant had known as a youngster when his father was playing in Italy and D'Antoni was a top player there, took his position. During their tenure with Team USA, D'Antoni and Bryant became great friends. Bryant joined Hall of Famers Chamberlain, Jordan, Kareem Abdul-Jabbar, and Karl Malone as one of five players to accomplish the milestone on December 5 against New Orleans, becoming him the youngest player (34 years and 104 days) in league history to do so. The longest streak by an NBA player after turning 34 was recorded by Bryant on December 18 in a 101-100 victory against the Charlotte Bobcats. It was also the fourth-longest stretch of its kind in his career. On December 28, he scored 27 points while sitting out the whole fourth quarter of a 104-87 victory against the Portland Trail Blazers, ending his streak at 10. D'Antoni started having Bryant cover the other team's top perimeter player to help the team's defense; Bryant was Kyrie Irving's main defender and kept him to 15 points. Bryant recognized that when he had a difficult defensive task as compared to when he played off the ball against inferior opponents, he was a more concentrated defender. By disrupting opponents, his defense allowed Nash to escape adverse situations.

For the majority of the first 42 games, Bryant had the highest scoring average in the league. After a dismal 17–25 start to the season, D'Antoni made Bryant the main offensive facilitator while moving Nash away from the ball to make him more of a spot-up shooter. Bryant recorded at least 10 assists in each of the next three victories, for a three-game total of 39 assists—the greatest in his career. With nine rebounds twice and eight the other time, he fell short of a triple-double in each game. He became the first Laker to achieve the feat since West in 1970 by scoring at least 40 points and dishing out at least 10 assists in back-to-back games in two key victories in March.

Bryant started playing almost all 48 minutes of every game as the Lakers battled for the eighth and final playoff spot in the Western Conference and dealt with ailments on the squad.

Bryant made NBA history on April 10, 2013, when he recorded the first-ever game with 47 points, 8 rebounds, 5 assists, 4 blocks, and 3 steals. Bryant's season was over when he tore his Achilles tendon on April 12 against the Golden State Warriors. His injury occurred after he had played at least 40 minutes for seven straight games and seven straight quarters. Only Portland rookie Damian Lillard averaged more minutes per game than the 34-year-old Bryant, who was playing his most games (38.6) in six years. Ten days before, Bryant had been speaking with Lakers general manager Mitch Kupchak about his heavy playing time, but Bryant felt the minutes needed to continue given the Lakers' playoff drive. In order to repair the damage, Bryant had surgery on April 13. It was anticipated that he would be out for six to nine months. He averaged 27.3 points, 46.3 percent shooting, 5.6 rebounds, and 6 assists per game as the season came to a close. The Lakers' return to the playoffs under his leadership was hailed by The New York Times as "perhaps some of his greatest work." During the season, he surpassed the 40-point mark eight times and had 10 or more assists 11 times in his position as a distributor. He was given the nickname "Magic Mamba" in honor of Magic Johnson's distributing prowess. Bryant's field goal percentage increased to its greatest level since 2008-09, while his assists were the second-most of his career. With a final record of 45-37, the Lakers were good for seventh place in the West. The San Antonio Spurs swept the Los Angeles Lakers in four games when they were playing without Bryant in the first round of the playoffs.

INJURY-PLAGUED YEARS (2013–2015)

Bryant started working out again in November 2013, well into the 2013–14 campaign. He agreed to a two-year contract deal with the Lakers on November 25 that was for an estimated $48.5 million. He continued to earn the most money in the league while accepting a reduced contract; he was qualified for an extension beginning at $32 million annually. Bryant's deal generated intense debate, with opponents saying that celebrities should accept lower salaries so that their teams would have more financial flexibility and supporters saying that the NBA's best players were being paid less than their real worth. Bryant missed the first 19 games of the season but started playing again on December 8. In a 96-92 victory against Memphis on December 17, Bryant equaled his season-high of 21 points, but he also sustained a lateral tibial plateau fracture in his left knee, which was projected to keep him out for six weeks. Since recovering from his Achilles injury, he has participated in six games, spending some of them at point guard due to Nash, Steve Blake, and Jordan Farmar's ailments. Averaging 13.8 points, 6.3 assists, and 4.3 rebounds per game, Bryant. He was benched, but fans chose for him to start in his 16th All-Star game. Some people compared Bryant's nomination to a lifetime accomplishment award for his prior success, but Bryant did not believe he was worthy of it. He was still constrained by his knee, therefore he didn't participate in the game. Bryant was declared out for the balance of the season by the Lakers on March 12, 2014, citing his need for more rehabilitation and the short season. The squad had a 22-42 record at the time, which was tied for the poorest mark in the Western Conference. The Lakers missed the playoffs for the first time since 2005 after finishing 27-55.

In his 19th season with the Lakers, Bryant returned for the 2014–15 campaign. The Lakers had Byron Scott, a former colleague of Bryant's, in place of D'Antoni. Bryant got his 20th triple-double in his career on November 30, 2014, in a 129-122 overtime win against the Toronto Raptors. He finished with 31 points, 12 assists, and 11 rebounds. He set an NBA record by recording 30 points, 10 rebounds, and 10 assists in a single game at the age of 36. In a 100-94 victory against Minnesota on December 14, Bryant passed Michael Jordan (32,292) to become the NBA's third-leading scorer all-time. In the first 27 games of the season, he participated, averaging a team-high 26.4 points and 35.4 minutes per game while also leading the league in shots attempted (22.4 per game). Bryant put on one of his worst performances of the season, committing nine turnovers and scoring 25 points on only 8 of 30 shooting in a 108-101 defeat to Sacramento.

As a result, Scott benched him for three consecutive games to give him some rest. Scott was experiencing pain in his back, foot, Achilles tendons, knees, and other areas, therefore he intended to reduce his workload moving ahead. Bryant had played more than 40 minutes three times, and the coach chastised himself for overloading him following his outstanding start to the season. Bryant had a season field goal percentage of only 37%, while the team's record was merely 8-19. He became only the third player in NBA history to post two triple-doubles in a season at age 36 or older with 23 points, 11 assists, and 11 rebounds in a 111-103 victory against Denver in his second game back after resting. Bryant tore the rotator cuff in his right shoulder on January 21, 2015, as he drove baseline for a two-handed slam against the New Orleans Pelicans. Despite being right-handed, he continued to participate in the game and handled the offense while mostly using his left hand for shooting, dribbling, and passing. Bryant has missed eight of the previous 16 games due to rest. After having surgery to treat the injury, he finished the season averaging 22.3 points but shooting a career-low 37.3 percent, far lower than his 45.4 percent lifetime average at the beginning of the season. His comeback was planned at the beginning of the 2015–16 season after a nine-month absence. The Lakers concluded the season with a record of 21-61, breaking the mark they had previously established for the most defeats in a season.

FINAL SEASON (2015-2016)

Bryant sustained a calf injury and missed the last two weeks of exhibition games in 2015-16 after recovering to play in the preseason. He nonetheless participated in the Lakers' season opening to start his 20th season with them, breaking John Stockton's previous record of 19 seasons spent with the same club. The Lakers' record dropped to 2-12 on November 24, 2015, following their 111-77 loss against the Warriors. Bryant's performance was the poorest of any game in which he took at least five shots, scoring only four points in 25 minutes on 1-for-14 shooting. The Lakers were defeated 103-91 by Bryant's hometown club, the Philadelphia 76ers, in his last game on December 1, 2015.

Bryant revealed through The Players' Tribune on November 29, 2015, that he will be retiring at the conclusion of the current campaign. Bryant said that he fell in love with basketball at the age of six in his poetry titled "Dear Basketball": "A love so deep I gave you my all/From my intellect & body/To my spirit & soul." 2015-2016 season "is all I have to offer. My body knows it's time to say goodbye, but my head and heart can manage the pressure. It's okay. I'm ready to let you go." Bryant penned the following in a letter sent to Lakers supporters before to that night's game against the Indiana Pacers: "More than whatever I've done for you, what you've done for me is far more significant. I will always cherish this city, this team, and everyone of you. I'm grateful for this amazing adventure."

He was averaging only 15.7 points per game, shooting a career-low 31.5 percent, and was second on the team in minutes (30.8) behind Jordan Clarkson. He also led the club with 16.7 field goal attempts per game at the time of his announcement. His long-range shooting and over-reliance on pump fakes had caused his free throw attempts to fall below career average, and he was hitting a league-worst 19.5 percent of his three-point tries despite making seven attempts a game, nearly twice his career average.

After the revelation, he admitted his deteriorating abilities in a press conference. "Despite the fact that I play poorly, I do my hardest to avoid doing so and I make every effort. And I appreciate that "he said.

Bryant asked visiting teams not to give him any presents in front of the crowd or have any on-court rituals in his honor. He had been certain before announcing his retirement that he did not want the bustle of a planned farewell tour, preferring to hear jeers rather than applause. Nevertheless, he received crowd ovations and video tributes from around the league, even in places where he had previously drawn jeers, including Boston's TD Garden, Philadelphia's Wells Fargo Center, Sacramento's Sleep Train Arena, and Salt Lake City's Vivint Smart Home Arena. Bryant was surprised by the applause that he was now getting since he had previously been respected but not liked.

Bryant beat the Minnesota Timberwolves 119-115 on February 3 thanks to seven three-pointers, a then-season-high 38 points, and 14 of the team's 18 points in the last 5:02 of the game. The Lakers avoided having their longest losing run in team history thanks to the victory, which snapped a 10-game losing skid. He became only the fourth player in NBA history over the age of 37 to record at least 35 points, five rebounds, and five assists in a single game. Stephen Curry received 1.6 million more votes than Bryant, who received 1.9 million, for the 2016 All-Star Game. Bryant was chosen as a frontcourt starter for the first time after switching to small forward for that season. Bryant scored 10 points, grabbed six rebounds, and handed out seven assists in his first All-Star game since 2013. In an effort to win him another All-Star MVP, West teammates tried to feed him the ball, but he rejected.

Bryant outscored the entire Jazz team 23-21 in the fourth quarter of the season finale on April 13 versus Utah, setting an NBA season best with 60 points. The Lakers went on to win 101-96. At 37 years and 234 days old, he set the record for the oldest player to score 60 or more points in a game. With a 17-65 record at the end of the season, the Lakers had their lowest record in company history.

MENTAL TOUGHNESS FOR SUCCESS

HOW TO SHOW RESPECT FOR WHAT YOU DO?

Once, Bryant had no sleep at all before he played a game. Zero sleep. This happened because one of the members of his family had a health situation. So he stood up all night, and he still had to go out and perform because fans and teammates don't care about your personal situation -and they shouldn't care that you've been up all night.

You've got to perform. You just have to go to work, no excuses. This is what respect for your profession is.

HOW TO USE YOUR NATURAL ADVANTAGES?

Bryant scored his first 60-point game when he was eight. He figured out at eight years old that other eight-year-olds couldn't dribble with their left hand. So it was something that was simple for him.

When he was guarding the ball, he always made sure he guarded the ball during that game. He'd always just let them have a couple dribbles with their right hand and then jump on their right hand and make them change it over to their left. And they would bobble the ball and fumble it. Bryant would pick it up and go lay it up. He just did that the whole game, and that's how he ended up at 63 points.

HOW TO PREPARE YOURSELF TO GAIN UNWAVERING CONFIDENCE?

Confidence comes from preparation. Bryant was sure there was no other way to gain confidence.

So when the game was on the line, he was not asking himself to do something that he hadn't done thousands of times before. When he prepared, he knew what he was capable of doing. He knew what he was comfortable doing and what he was not comfortable doing.

If your job, like Bryant's, is to try to be the best basketball player you can be, you have to do that too. You have to practice, you have to train. You want to train as much as you can, as often as you can. So, if you wake up at 10, train at 11, train at 12, train for two hours, from 12 to two.

Then, you have to let your body recover. So you eat, recover, and do what you have to do. You get back out, you train again. Afterwards, you go home, you shower, you eat dinner, you go to bed, you wake up, and you do it all over again. R

Now, imagine that, instead of waking up at 11, you wake up at three, you train at four, so you go from four to six, then come home, have breakfast, and relax. Then you're back at it again, nine to 11. You relax again until, all of a sudden, you're back at it again, two to four, and now you're at it again, seven to nine.

Look how much more training you could do by simply starting at four. Actually, this was Bryant's routine, and anyone disciplined enough can follow it.

WHAT IS THE BLACK MAMBA MENTALITY?

Once Bryant made that commitment and said, "I want to be one of the greatest ever," the game became everything for him. This is when he created the black mamba mentality.

The key factor for him wasn't whether or not he was ready. It was the fact that if he wasn't ready, he was determined to figure out how to get ready. And ultimately, even if he was ready, he still needed to improve. So the work's not going to stop.

Bryant believed that greatness is not something that lives and dies with one person. It's how you inspire a person to then, in turn, inspire another person to inspire another person -and so the inspiration goes on forever. According to Bryant, that's how you leave a positive mark in the world for the rest of time.

MENTAL TOUGHNESS FOR PRODUCTIVITY

WHY YOU SHOULD MEDITATE EVERYDAY?

Bryant used to meditate every day. He did it in the mornings for about 10 to 15 minutes. He thought that was important because it just set him up for the rest of the day -it helped him. For him, it was like having an anchor, and if he didn't do it, he would feel like he was constantly chasing the day as opposed to being able to control and dictate the day.

If he didn't meditate, he couldn't call the shots on what came forward. However, most of the time he felt like he was set and ready for whatever may come his way; he had a calmness about whatever came his way -and a poise. He believed that came from starting the morning off with meditation.

HOW TO HAVE THE MOST PRODUCTIVE DAY?

Bryant used to get up at four thirty in the morning after he got injured, even if he didn't have to train anymore. So at what time did he go to sleep?

He said he didn't need too many hours of sleep. He could go off for just three or four hours.

What was a normal day like for him? Particularly in the off season, when he got up at about four thirty in the morning, he would get ready to work out. Off season was past summer, so he couldn't run like he normally did and do all the shots because of his knee.

So he would get up in the morning and do his therapy, do weights, and other things of that nature. He would do that about twice, three times a day sometimes. He said that the key is, when you get up that early in the morning, to finish your workout at 12 o'clock, or 12:30, so that you can have the rest of the day to kick it with the fan -and recover if you are injured and your body needs it.

Instead of waking up in the middle of the day, you get all of those hours in, then your day gets the most productive it can be.

Bryant believed he did not become so successful just because of talent or ability. He says it was because he got up at 4:00 AM, and he did it because of two things. Some days, he would be up early because he had a dream and he would let nothing stand in his way. If anything tried to bring him down, he used it to make him stronger. He was never satisfied, and he was never finished.

HOW TO TRAIN MORE DURING THE DAY?

You have to let your body recover. So you eat, recover, and when you get back out, you train. You start training at six, then you go home, you shower, you eat dinner. You go to bed, you wake up and do it again.

That was Bryant's routine, but he did it earlier and repeated it throughout the day: He woke up at three, he trained at four, he went from four to six, came home, had breakfast, and relaxed. Then he was back at it again from nine to 11. He relaxed and then, all of a sudden, he was back at it again, two to four. He was back to it again seven to nine. Look how much more training you can do by simply starting at four.

DOES EFFORT EVER STOP?

Bryant would go out with this team and drink with them. But the next morning, he would be banging on their doors at five in the morning to say, "Let's go. The competition is not getting where we're going. I'll hang out with you. Now you come hang out with me."

Then, at the gym, they would work out and go to practice. They could go out that night or play a game, but the next morning they had to start all over again.

WHAT IS THE ZONE OF DEEP CONCENTRATION?

Did Bryant ever get distracted? Would he get distracted if he saw Rihanna and Ciara sitting courtside? Being totally honest, his answer was "No."

To him, the game was the only thing that mattered in the world. When he was playing, he was about his business. He couldn't even notice anyone, no matter who was present in the courtside.

The only thing Bryant noticed before every game was when he looked up at those championship bands. He said that when you get in the zone like that, you just get supreme confidence that you're going to win.

He said that, in the zone, everything slows down. You're still you; you just have supreme confidence. But when that happens, you really do not try to focus on what's going on -you feel like you are on your own, and you just kind of stay there and become oblivious.
Everything that's going on around you disappears, except for the game itself.

WHY SLEEPING WELL IS ESSENTIAL FOR PERFORMANCE?

When he was younger, Bryant's sleep habits were horrendous, to say the least. He had always had a hard time sleeping. He just couldn't figure out how to shut his brain off. So what made the light bulb come on is that he went out there and played a game -and he played like crap. He thought to himself, "Why am I playing like crap?"

He realized it was because he had been practicing the same moves over and over and over, but he couldn't execute them properly yet. He was feeling sluggish, he was feeling lethargic, and he knew it wasn't because of his training; he had trained obsessively.

It dawned on him that maybe he wasn't playing well because of the fact that he was sleeping only two or three hours a night..

WHY SHOULD YOU BE FOREVER A STUDENT?

With the amount of success he had, how could Bryant remain so humble?

In Bryant's own words: "I'm a student. "He never considered himself the master of anything. He said he had to constantly learn. His mantra was to value growth, because in order to grow, you have to constantly learn. You have to constantly move, constantly improve. To Bryant, that was the key that made life fun.

For instance, Bryant loves to call people he knew and asked them, "What did you read recently? What did you learn? How did you learn it?"

If you have the love to always be learning, you'll be able to handle whatever bumps come your way.

MENTAL TOUGHNESS FOR OVERCOMING STRUGGLE

HOW TO USE YOUR STRUGGLES TO SHAPE YOUR GOALS?

Bryant always had one powerful purpose: he wanted to be one of the best basketball players to ever play. Anything else that was outside of that lane, he didn't have time for.

At what age did that goal become his? He was crystal clear that that's what he was and he made that deal with himself at 13 years old.

That meant taking things and using things in his life that were scars; he used those moments as a weapon, a vehicle for expressing himself through basketball.

This is why, at any given moment, to face another team was not about the other team, according to Bryant. It's not about your opponent. It's about you. It's about you taking your inner struggles and channeling them through the game as a means of emancipation.

So the question you have to ask is: how do I express that to my opponent?

HOW TO USE YOUR SUFFERING TO CREATE YOUR KILLER INSTINCT?

Where did Bryant get his killer instinct from?

Bryant thought that a lot of it had to do with growing up in Italy and being the only African American kid, and not being able to speak the language. This made him gravitate towards the game. And in that game, he found a lot of solace.

He said that when you play with kids that might not accept you because you're an outsider, things might get harder. But yet, when Bryant and the other kids played the game, that was his chance to get vengeance on them for not accepting him.

That's where his killer instinct started developing. Throughout the course of his life, Bryant always felt like he was the outsider, having to come in and prove himself, or to seek some sort of vengeance.

HOW TO HAVE YOUR HEAD IN THE GAME?

Bryant suggested you do the following imagination exercise.

Imagine you just had an injury in the hamstring and the doctor tells you to go home, sit up on the couch, and massage your hamstring. Don't get up. No sudden movements.

When you're at home, all of a sudden, a fire breaks out. Your kids are upstairs. Your wife is wherever she may be. Your house is going down and you're injured. Bryant was willing to bet that you're going to forget about your hamstring.

You're going to sprint upstairs. You're going to grab your kids and make sure your wife's good. You're getting out of that house - hamstring be damned. You're not going to stretch your hamstrings.

The reason is that the lives of your family are more important than the injury to your hamstring. And so when the game is more important than the injury itself, you don't feel that damn injury. Not at that time.

HOW TO KEEP GOING?

Even after retiring from his basketball career, Bryant believed he was far from done. His next dream was to be honored one day for inspiring the next generation. He believed that athletes who have a dream must sacrifice for it and never ever rest in the middle of their journey.

He firmly said, "Always keep going. Regardless, the storm eventually ends. And when a storm does end, you want to make sure that you're ready."

So if you're going to do something, do it to the best of your ability. No matter what it is.

CAN LONELINESS BE A GOOD THING?

When Bryant was 17 years old, he wasn't invited to parties or any friendly gatherings on the weekend. So, on Fridays and Saturdays, he would go in his room with his basketball and basically dribble himself to sleep. He thought that that was the best thing that could have ever happened to him.

Because during those lonely hours in the room, he discovered the hunger, the motivation, and the will to be the best possible basketball player that he could be.

HOW TO CHANGE YOUR PERSPECTIVE WHEN YOU SUFFER BECAUSE THINGS DON'T GO YOUR WAY?

When his team seemed like a hot mess, Bryant made an effort to have perspective. He believed that sometimes you can look clearly at things and see why they are going in a horrible direction. He said most people want to overreact to that, because when things go really wrong, everything feels so massive -and so they start struggling.

This happened to the Lakers when they were playing good basketball. Everybody was like, "Oh my God, the Lakers are really shocking people. Oh, what they're doing is unbelievable." Then an injury would happen, and then another injury would happen.

To keep things in perspective when those things happened, Bryant went back to the thought that the worst thing that can happen to anyone is to stop walking the earth, so he would tell everyone to relax, even if they were not going to make the playoffs.

Once, in the critical part of the season, half the team was gone due to injuries. What are you supposed to do with that? There was nothing they could do except to just settle down and enjoy their time.

Once they went back into championships, they could look back at that time of injury with joy because it made championships much sweeter.

MENTAL TOUGHNESS FOR LEADERSHIP

HOW CAN A BASKETBALL TEAM BE GOOD?

Who's the toughest guy Bryant ever played against? The guy that always gave him the most problems was actually Tracy McGrady. There was something about Tracy that Bryant always found fascinating; he had all the skills and all the athleticism, and he was really, really tough to figure out.

However, for Bryant, there was no victory by defeating just one guy. The important thing was defeating a good team.

Bryant believed that, to win a championship, a team cannot rely on a style of play that consists of only one player dominating the ball. A team needs to have more movement in the office, where they move guys around, where they're harder to find.

If you take one player, you put them at the top of the key or you put them on the wing, you're doing a screen roll and you're always in front of the defense. The defense can key on that.

HOW TO HANDLE A TEAM'S STUBBORNNESS?

Bryant would always tell the guys that they had to go back to back.

He didn't care if they were in Miami. He didn't care if they were in the great city of Chicago- they couldn't go out because they needed to get some rest after playing back-to-back games.

However, he said the guys didn't listen to him one time. They said to him, "We'll all go out together anyway." So what Bryant did was join them for a drink, but he warned them: "The next morning, I'm banging on your door at five in the morning. Let's go. I'll hang out with you. But then you come hang out with me." And that is what they did.

Next morning, they were at the gym working out, like Bryant said they had to. Then they hit the bus and went to practice. They played that night, and all the team was dead.

Bryant said it was a lesson learned. Bryant said that, if you're a leader, and your team wants to do something contrary to what you say, let them do it once, but don't let that compromise what they're here to do.

WHY LET OTHERS USE THEIR STRENGTHS EVEN WHEN YOU'RE GOOD ENOUGH?

What did Bryant learn from Bill Russell? Bryant was always geeked out about the game, so practically speaking, Bryant learned to use his strengths and let others use theirs.

Once, Russell told him, "When I played, I could score the ball, I could handle the ball, and I could pass the ball, but it was really important for me to look at my teammates and say, 'Okay, there are other players here that do that better. Therefore, I must allow them to do that.' And what I do best is defend and rebound. So I'm going to completely focus on that. Let Cozi handle the ball, right? Let Sam be the shooter."

Bryant thought that was a very, very insightful piece of advice, which he later used in how he was able to go on and win those two championships with his team.

WHY MUST A LEADER BE COMPASSIONATE AND EMPATHETIC?

What did Bryant know and learn at the end of his career that he wished he had known at the beginning?

His answer was empathy and compassion. As a young kid, when he came into a league, he felt it was like either being on the train or being on the track; there was no such thing as understanding that people have lives outside of the game -which he apparently did not have.

If he had understood at an early age, it would have helped him as a leader to communicate. However, he did come to understand that later. Getting to know people on a personal level, their fears, their insecurities, their dreams and ambitions, and desires, finally made him empathetic.

Compassion and empathy are needed in a person who can help others achieve the best version of themselves.

HOW CAN A TEAM BE GOOD YEAR AFTER YEAR?

What did the Lakers need to do to get better every year for the next year? In Bryant's simple words, they just had to continue to work. The individual players had to go in the direction the team decided to go, whether it was a big-time free agent, whether it was a trade with the young pieces that they had, whatever the case may be.

If the team decided to keep the young talent, they had to start going to the gym immediately and put the work in right away. The team had to figure out how it could use each other to be more efficient on both ends of the basketball court. It was this same process every year.

When anyone looks at Bryant's career, it can be clearly noticed that there were a lot of times when he had to carry a team.

Bryant said that wasn't that hard at all, because he had a chance to work with people that thought the same way and had the same kind of passion. That way, they all created together a beautiful environment to work in.

WHY MUST YOU BE HONEST WITH PEOPLE?

Bryant saw the movie *Whiplash*, and he agreed with a phrase one of the characters said: the worst thing that you can say to somebody, as far as motivation goes, and as far as helping somebody to improve, is they're doing a good job when they didn't do a good job.

Bryant identified with JK Simmons' character in that way. He said that if someone did something and it was not very well done, he was not going to say it was well done. From time to time, Bryant would verbally slap a teammate and tell him what he was doing wrong.

That way, people also knew that when he said something, he meant it.

For instance, if someone was having lunch or having dinner with Bryant and they were sitting across from him and had something in their teeth, Bryant wouldn't have evaded the uncomfortable moment and he would have told the person they had something in their teeth.

HOW MUST A LEADER TRAIN THEIR TEAM?

Bryant thought practice was important, not only from the standpoint that he enjoyed playing -he had a good time and he enjoyed getting better-, but as a leader of a team.

As a leader, it's your responsibility to elevate the rest of the guys. What people tend to get stuck on a lot is saying, "Okay, the way to make players better is to pass them the ball when they're open." To Bryant, that's a very trivial way to look at it.

What you have to do is you have to get them emotionally to want to be better. You have to get them to an emotional space where they wake up every morning, driven to be the best version of themselves. And how do you do that?

In practice, it was an opportunity for Bryant to push them, to challenge them. This is where you have to know your teammates, because if it was late, they would just have a back to back and had practice the next day, because the guys wouldn't feel like going through the motions, and wouldn't feel like practicing.

It's important to know each and every one of your team members individually and personally, because then you can be totally honest with them without hurting their feelings. With some guys, you've got to figure out what button to push. You have to drive them. You absolutely have to. And if practice is more intense and hard, then the next game will be easier -but if it's not, then that's when teams start folding and capping.

CONSISTENCY

HOW TO GAIN REAL CONSISTENCY?

Bryant's consistency of work is: Monday, get better; Tuesday, get better; Wednesday, get better; Thursday, get better, etc. He says that, if you want a high level of performance, you have to do that over a period of time, not like one month or two months -it's 3, 4, 5, 6, 7, 8, 9, 10 years. And then you get to where you want to go.

Always keep going. There were times in Bryant's career, particularly early on, when he felt like the end was near. But what he came to find out is that, no matter what happens, the storm eventually ends. And when a storm does end, you want to make sure that you're ready.

WHY REST AT THE END?

Rest at the end, not in the middle. That's something Bryant always lived by. He never went to rest. He kept on pushing. There were a lot of answers that he didn't have or even questions that he didn't have, but he kept going. He just kept going until he figured these things out. He just continued to build that way, and he tried to live by that all the time.

Bryant's high school English teacher, Mr. Fisk, once told him a beautiful quote about resting at the end, not in the middle. And Bryant took that to heart. He believed there is a time for resting at the end, but that time was not near for him because he had a dream to sacrifice for, and he would never rest in the middle.
Rest at the end. There's no end goal.

WHAT IS COMMITMENT?

After he retired, Bryant started writing. He wanted to understand how to tell stories. He started reading Joseph Campbell on how to create compelling arcs and plots -he was actually reading on technical advice.

He eventually wrote and created the animated film *Dear Basketball*, a project he said came from hard work and from studying for 15 years; it came from knowing how to write and how to organize structure. Bryant said you can't do that without having a serious love or commitment to the craft.

DO YOU NEED CONSTANT MENTORSHIP TO BE SUCCESSFUL?

Did Bryant have friends? Did he have guys he could hang out with? His answer was, "No, I do not have any friends. Zero.

Bryant once said he hated people. Was Michael Jordan a friend of his? Well, not exactly, but he was a good mentor to Bryant . Actually, he was like a big brother to him. How regularly would Bryant speak to Michael? He said that maybe once a year, or every once in a while. But that was enough to get good quality mentorship.

Growing up, Bryant's idol and mentor was Magic Johnson, who he greatly admired. And then, of course, he was one of the team's owners.

Later on, one of his mentors became Shaquille O'Neal, with whom he had an up and down relationship. O'Neal said that Bryant was the greatest Laker of all time. Did Bryant agree with that? What did that mean to him? Bryant said, "Well, I'll never disagree with my elders. No, I'm kidding."

FAILURE

WHAT IS FAILURE?

Basketball, for Bryant, was the most important thing. Everything he did was done to try to learn how to have that point of view. Literally.

So what did "failure" mean for Bryant? To him, it didn't exist. Bryant said failure is a figment of your imagination. So if you fail today, you have to decide to progress from that. Because if you fail today, you're going to learn something from that failure. And you'll be trying again tomorrow.

Bryant said his brain couldn't process failure. It just would not process failure. Because if he had to, if he sat there and had to face himself and tell himself, "You're a failure," that, he believed, was worse than anything else in the world.

HOW TO RECOVER FROM FAILURE?

Bryant felt like everybody had written him off after shooting a series of airballs. However, failure was something that neither his brain nor his heart could process.

When he got home -it was probably like three in the morning- he went down to the high school. The janitor led him to the gym, and he shot all day, right after that playoff game. He just kept shooting and shooting and shooting. He kept practicing and practicing, because that's the only way you can fight off failure.

You just have to keep going no matter what. If you've failed ten times now, the eleventh time will be fantastic. It's bound to happen. That time, Bryant got a chance to let out the steam of disappointing his teammates and millions of fans.

PASSION

WHY MUST YOU DO WHAT YOU LOVE TO DO?

According to Bryant, the trick to enjoying what you do is finding what you love to do. We talk about hard work all the time, and it's like, but if you've got to get up every single morning and remind yourself how hard you need to work, you probably need to choose a different profession.

That reluctance shouldn't be there. Bryant used to wake up excited to get to it in the morning. If he was not training, he was missing it. If he was not watching that game of basketball, he was missing it. To him, there was no place he'd rather be.

So if you have that same feeling, then you are truly doing what God has put in your heart.

WHAT TO DO WHEN YOU RETIRE?

Once you retire, you don't have that source of income that's coming in. So even if you save over a 15-year career, if your spending habits remain the same, eventually that well is going to run dry.

Unfortunately for athletes, the retirement age is 32. If you're lucky, you could retire at 37, like Bryant. But still, what comes next?

The question is, what happens next? What should you do? What is your passion? Bryant said it's not where you can add the most value or make the most money. What you have to wonder is, what is your next passion? When you find that next passion, everything else will make sense.

HOW TO MAKE YOUR DREAMS COME TRUE?

Making a dream come true, according to Bryant, is about those times when you get up early and you work hard; those times when you stay up late and you work hard; those times when you don't feel like working; you're too tired; you don't want to push yourself, but you do it anyway. That is actually the dream. That's the dream. It's not the destination. It's the journey.

And if you can understand that, then what you'll see happen is that you won't accomplish your dreams; they won't come true. Something greater will.

HOW TO STICK TO YOUR DREAMS?

The lesson Bryant cherished the most is how important it is to love what you do. All the hard work and perseverance will pay off if you love what you do and it's making you happy.

Bryant once had a guidance counselor tell him that he shouldn't play basketball, that it would never amount to anything. However, that counselor's negativity towards him made him stronger.

Bryant said that you can't stop people from trying to limit your dreams, but you can stop them from becoming a reality. Your dreams are up to you. Bryant encouraged everyone to always be curious, always seek out things they love, and always work hard once they find them.

HOW TO CHOOSE YOUR FUTURE WISELY BASED ON YOUR PASSION?

The process Bryant went through to come to the decision of making himself eligible for the NBA draft wasn't easy.

Playing in the NBA had always been a goal of Bryant. Back then, he was basically going through the high school seats and trying to think if that was really what he wanted to do -if college was a place that he wanted to skip, if that experience was worth taking ahead of the NBA.

That's what he was mainly trying to focus on. Back when he was in ninth grade, he had already made the decision that, if it were possible, he would skip college and go right to playing professional basketball. He just wanted to give himself the option to either go to the NBA or go to college. And he worked very hard to make that goal possible.

Part of what made that unique is that his father played in the NBA as well, and he certainly influenced Bryant in at least part of his decision. His father gave him a lot of pros and cons, even though the game had changed a lot since his father's time. For instance, the total attitudes and the money of the game had totally changed since then, but still, his father was able to give him a pretty good feel for it.

A lot of people wondered why the rush: Bryant was only 17 years old and he could still go to college and get one year in. Besides, he came from a middle-class family, so why jump college?

Bryant loved the competition, and while college was great competition, the NBA had the best players in the world. He simply adored the game, and the chance to be amongst the best players in the world.

Right from the start, Bryant knew that he was going to work extremely hard. If he wasn't an instant success, then he knew he would have to work harder. He knew he was not the only one coming out of high school to apply for the NBA draft.

In the end, Bryant was 110% confident that playing basketball was what he wanted to do, no matter what.

TRANSCENDENCE

DO YOU NEED COMPLIMENTS TO KNOW THAT YOU'RE DOING SOMETHING WORTHY?

Bryant was once asked that, if he were to receive a compliment from one player in the league, whose compliment would mean the most to him?

His answer was that he didn't really care about any of them. To him, they had all just wound up together trying to create something that was going to inspire someone, maybe in future generations.

What Bryant came to learn as his career went on is that that was more significant than any championship. That's why he was consumed with this quest to try to be the best.

Bryant always thought the definition of greatness was to inspire the next generation, and that's something only young people can say whether it's happening or not. Empty compliments prove nothing.

HOW TO DO SOMETHING TRANSCENDENTAL?

Something that Bryant always tried to do was to ask questions. He thought that when you understand why things happen, then you can understand how to make things happen.

And for Bryant, the most important question he could ask himself was: "How can you inspire a person who then, in turn, inspires another person?"

For Bryant, the answer to that question is how you create something that lasts forever.

WHY THINKING ABOUT YOUR MORTALITY MAKES YOU WISER?

Do athletes have an acceptance of their mortality? Bryant believed the best ones did. He thought that, if you combat it, you'll always have that inner struggle within yourself. Bryant himself was comfortable with his mortality.

When Bryant injured his Achilles tendon, he knew his recovery couldn't be immediate -and that it could mean the end of his career. However, he didn't take it too badly thanks to his ideas around mortality: if your life can end at any moment, so can all your goals, careers or material things.

Instead of freaking out, he decided to use his recovery time to come up with new ideas and new businesses, which became very successful eventually. It was all very exciting for him, because it was the process of starting a new chapter.

Bryant never focused on not being depressed. He focused on the excitement of building something new.

What was Bryant's relationship with death? It was a comfortable one. To Bryant, it was an agreement. You can't have life without death; you can't have light without the dark -his relationship with death was an acceptance of that.

It came around the time to decide whether or not he should retire.

MOTIVATION

HOW TO GIVE YOUR ALL?

When Bryant went to Orlando while he was trying to win his championships in LA, he absolutely buried himself even more so in the craft and literally cut everybody out of hIs life to just focus on that. He remembers feeling such a sense of joy because of what he was doing. There was also a sense of pride.

If your job is to try to be the best basketball player you can be, Bryant said you have to practice, you have to train as much as you can, as often as you can. So, if you wake up at 10, train at 11 or train at 12. Do it for two hours at least.

WHY ARE DREAMS SO IMPORTANT?

How did Bryant stretch his beliefs to make sure he was continually pushing the boundaries of his comfort zone and his capabilities?

Bryant said he just dreamed. He had dreams -and he said dreams should be pure. He thought a lot of times that, when we're born into this world, you actually wind up going backwards. It seemed to him that the more we mature, the more responsible our dreams are.

SHOULD YOUR OPPONENTS BE GREAT TOO?

Who's the toughest guy Bryant ever played against?

The answer is he didn't have one single most difficult opponent he ever faced; it depended on the situation.

However, Bryant did admit there was a stretch where Allen Iverson was just a pain to deal with. According to Bryant, he was really, really tough, and there was a game where he dropped 44 on him in Philadelphia.

There was another game in New Jersey where Marbury dropped 50 on Bryant. And there was yet another game where Carmelo Anthony dropped 70. Anthony was always tough for Bryant to deal with. Keevin Durant was always tough to deal with too.

So Bryant had a lot of great rivals, but the guy that always gave him the most problems was actually Tracy McGrady. Bryant said that there was something special about Tracy McGrady that made him have all the skills and all the athleticism to win; he was really, really tough to figure out.

WHY CAN STORIES CHANGE OUR LIVES?

What obsesses Bryant over besides playing basketball? Well, he absolutely loved storytelling; for me, it was the number one thing. He loved to outline and create narratives that could inspire the next generation of athletes, from a fantasy and a mythology perspective.

He always wondered: What are those stories that we can use to teach the next generation of athletes? Not just about the sport, but teach them about life through sport. How do we make those connections? And so that's what he obsessed over every single day.

What was his favorite type of mythology? Bryant grew up studying Greek mythology at a very early age, which he thought was kind of weird. At the age of 10, in Italy, in his class, they actually had to read the Iliad in Latin and be able to recite verses from it. He didn't realize how strange that was at 10 until he went back to the United States, and nobody else knew how to recite those verses.

The thing that Bryant gravitated to was the difference between Achilles and Hector, and the different philosophies that they both embodied. They had very contrasting beliefs, and so Bryant wondered: In whom did he see himself more?

Even at that early age, he thought Achilles was more interesting, because he was more aggressive; he was not bound to the limitations from others' perspective of him. Those were very complex and complicated issues for a kid at 10 to start understanding, of course. But Bryant thought that the sooner we can teach kids those types of lessons in a way that's easily digestible for them, in a way that's entertaining and fun for them, the sooner they can start striving for their own definition of excellence.

LIFESTYLE

SHOULD YOU PRIORITIZE YOUR PERSONAL LIFE OVER YOUR PROFESSION?

Was there ever any chance that Bryant could have been involved with the Lakers' organization as a coach, or a manager? His answer was always No because he was busy enough, although the Lakers would always be a part of him.

Bryant liked his free time; he didn't want to have to go to games, he didn't want to have to go to everything.

Instead, he enjoyed taking his wife to the movies. He enjoyed taking his family out to lunch. He enjoyed giving Bianka, his daughter, a shower every night. Those were his favorite parts, and he didn't want to give that up. He was at least always a phone call away. He had opened up the fact that fatherhood was an amazing thing.

Bryant liked to control his own schedule. That way, he could coach his daughters and be president at all of his eldest daughter's volleyball games.

His daughters practiced two hours a day and they were fully committed to their teammates, as well as to playing. Bryant enjoyed watching them play. It was fun because he got to see their growth, since when they first started and were not able to dribble the ball and walk at the same time, to the point they played like pros, grasping really complicated concepts and just reading and reacting on their own. It was entertaining to watch.

WHY MUST YOU SAVE A LOT OF MONEY AT THE PEAK OF YOUR CAREER?

Bryant saved a lot of money during the peak of his career. He did well, and here's why.

Bryant gave this advice to a lot of athletes who got paid by big endorsements: once you retire, you won't have the source of income that's coming in right now. So, even if you save over a 15-year career, your spending habits will remain the same. Eventually, that well is going to run dry. Unfortunately for athletes, the retirement age is 32. You're lucky if you manage to retire at 37, like Bryant.

So the question needs to be, "What comes next? What can I do? What is my passion?" The question shouldn't be where you can create the most value or generate the most revenue, but what your next passion is. Once you find that next passion, Bryant said everything else will make sense. But that's the hardest part for anyone, and that's also why you need to save enough, so that you can devote time to finding your true passions.

CHILDREN

WHY SPORTS ARE SO IMPORTANT FOR CHILDREN?

Bryant thought it was extremely important that kids stayed in sports. Why?

According to him, playing a sport teaches you a lot of valuable lessons, aside from the physical effort; and aside from the mental health benefits that you get from playing sports.

Bryant thought there's also an emotional component to sports. He believed sports are the greatest metaphor we have for life, in teaching you things like how to deal with anxiety, how to deal with communicating with each other, leadership, performing under pressure, and many other very valuable lessons.

This is why this topic became something that he really became passionate about. He started to find out ways to make games more engaging, and how to enable kids to play. He believed we live now in an environment where everything is extremely structured for children -but sports used to be something that kids would go out and do for fun.

Now, sports have become so regimented, that parents are starting to inject their experiences or past failures onto their children -and it just takes the fun out of it. Parents are highly influential in what children do.

The lessons Bryant tried to pass on are: one, children have to get to know each other, and try to build a bond, like a sisterhood or a brotherhood. Two, the game should be fun.

HOW TO ENGAGE CHILDREN IN SPORTS?

So how did Bryant attract children's curiosity? How did he get them interested in the sport? How did he teach children the game versus barking out instructions?
First of all, he said that when you get children to think in order to start to problem solve on their own, the game becomes something that they own and something that becomes more enjoyable to them.

To achieve this, parents must never bark out orders. Helicopter parents have exactly that say-so.

Also, Bryant said youth sports have changed over the years. Years ago, when he was younger, seeing and playing sports was just for fun. Unfortunately, now it has gotten to a point where it's basically a business, so a lot of kids don't have the opportunity to let their bodies heal. They don't have the opportunity to really grow as basketball players or as athletes because of all the pressure that's being put on them. Bryant thought it had been going downhill for quite a while.

So how can coaches do a better job when they have to train children? First, they have to acknowledge that kids are actually under their wings. Training kids shouldn't be about winning or losing a game. In fact, it has nothing to do with games. At this stage, it's really about helping individual children get better: How do you, as a coach, help them to become better people and better athletes? If the coach can remove themselves from that equation and just focus on teaching, then kids' experience will be much better.

HOW TO TEACH KIDS EXCELLENCE?

Bryant always tried to teach kids what excellence looks like.

Some of the kids he trained wanted to play in the NBA some day, some of them didn't. Either way, he tried to give them a foundation of the amount of work and preparation that it takes to be excellent in whatever it is that they choose to do.

This is why he helped them focus on the details of basketball. He also helped children learn the basics and the fundamentals. They would go over those things over and over, hoping it was something that they could apply to other areas in their life.

Actually, Bryant's daughter wanted to play in the NBA; Bryant thought it was the best thing. Sometimes, when he went out with her, fans would come up to Bryant to tell him, "Hey, you've got to have a boy. You and your wife have got to have a boy. Man, you need to have somebody who carries on the tradition, the legacy." Bryant's daughter would be listening, and she would say, "I got this. I will carry his legacy."

THIS IS THE END
OF THE PUBLICATION.

COPYRIGHT

LEGAL DISCLAIMER

This book aims to provide information and entertainment to its readers. The author has used reliable sources for the content, but cannot guarantee its accuracy or validity and is not responsible for any errors or omissions.

The book is not intended to be professional advice and should not replace the guidance of experts. The reader should consult professionals before using any protocols or medical treatments described in the book.

The reader agrees to use the information in the book at their own risk and the author is not liable for any costs, expenses, damages, or professional fees that may arise from using the information in the book. This disclaimer applies to any direct or indirect use of the information, and the author is not liable for any damages, negligence, criminal intent or other causes of action.

REVIEWS

We hope that this book has been helpful in providing a deeper understanding and analysis of the subject.

We appreciate your time in reading and hope that you found the content useful.

If you enjoyed the book, we would be grateful if you could leave a positive review, as this is one of the ways for new authors like us to gain visibility and improve the quality of our writing.

Thank you for your support!

Kobe Bryant Mentality: Become As Relentless As A Black Mamba By Decoding The Psychology Of A Legendary Laker: Kobe Bryant
by ETERNIA PUBLISHING

Author: ETERNIA PUBLISHING
Contact: (contact@eterniapublishing.com)

If you liked the book, recommend your friends to download their own copy, thank you very much for respecting the author's work!